Meditations with Saint Julian of Norwich

Madonna Sophia Compton

Also by Madonna Sophia Compton:
Women Saints: 365 Daily Readings
Prayers of the Saints
Sophia-Spirit-Mary
Odes of Solomon (inclusive language)
Sisters in Wisdom
The Transcendent Feminine
More Glorious than the Seraphim

Meditations with..... (series)

Meditations with Saint Julian of Norwich

This book is dedicated to my friend,

Huli Tabone

Special thanks to Sr. Therese and

Sr. Cornelia of the Order of

St. Julian of Norwich

Part 1:

Julian of Norwich: Her Life in Context

Julian of Norwich: Her Life in Context

Julian of Norwich is one of the most popular Christian women read and translated in both academic and devotional circles today. Although we don't know anything about Julian's prior life, she lived as an anchorite for many years in a small room attached to a church at Norwich. Besides her contemplation and writing, Julian was well known as a mystic and spiritual counselor and she was frequently visited by clergy and lay persons alike. Sometime during her life, she had what we would today call a Near-death Experience, when she received a series of visions, which she would reflect on for the rest of her life.

Julian lived in 14th century England during horrific conditions of plagues and wars. In the midst of such great suffering many in her own village, whom Julian herself would have undoubtedly known, died; it is possible that Julian lost some of her own family members. The Black Death had been imported from the continent in 1348 and it reached Norwich the following year. Julian would have been 6 or 7 years of age. People died miserable deaths in great numbers. Most could not be buried with dignity. By the end of this wave, more than 1/3 of the population had been decimated, including 50% of the clergy who administered to them and were therefore at higher risk. There was another wave of the Black Death when Julian was in her teens. Julian does not speak of the plague directly in her writings —or any other social or political event. But her writing shows a deep sensitivity to suffering and dying.

The country was also in a serious famine by 1369, when Julian would have been a young woman of 19. Tensions mounted as landlords tried to keep serfs tied to their old terms of service and an open revolt occurred with peasants in rebellion against their lords. One rebel band was led by Geoffrey Litster of Norwich. In 1377 the Great Schism occurred in the Roman Church, an unholy spectacle that resulted in mutual excommunications. Julian grew up, indeed, in very troubled times, which makes the positive tone of her writings all the more remarkable. As death was a daily occurrence, Julian did not hesitate to acknowledge that, since humanity's falling, we live in a time of suffering; but at the same time, her theology focuses on the depth of God's love, and the great joy in encountering it.

During Julian's time, the town of Norwich had a house of Beguines—the only English city to do so. The Beguinages were semi-monastic houses for self-organized sisterhoods which had grown up in various places in Europe, primarily the Low Countries during the middle ages. They were composed of women who did not want to marry nor join a convent and offered their self-supporting services to the community in the form of orphanages, hospices and schools for girls. By the 14th century, they were beginning to be persecuted by the hierarchy of the church for suspected heresies, since a number of them, like Julian, were mystics who wrote about their visionary encounters with Christ, and many of them disseminated their teachings without the approval of their local priests, or confessors.

Julian would have been aware that some of these women were being investigated and she mentions several times in her initial writings that she fully accepts ecclesiastical authority. After she recovered from her serious illness, Julian wrote down her experiences in what is known as the *Short Text,* and around 20 years later she expanded her reflections and her theology about the nature of God and the soul in the *Long Text.* The apparent self-doubt and concern over her ability to teach because she is a woman is expressed in the *Short Text*, but are not present in the *Long Text.* In the space between the two writings, Julian seems to have gained confidence in her own authority; in her second text she seems clear about the fact that her theology is based on her own spiritual experiences and insights. At the same time, Julian shows herself to be a woman of profound intellect and has often been ranked with Chaucer as a pioneering genius of English prose.

There is material in Julian's writing, for example her theory of universal salvation, that would be considered radical, even by many in today's standards. Julian's is not a systematic theology that one would see emerge from the pen of a male speculative mystic like Meister Eckhart or Bonaventure. Julian' s mystical experience is, like St. Paul's on the road to Damascus, very personal. In this regard we should note that a feminine way of doing theology is often a reflection of how our personal experience informs our theology. Julian definitely grew to trust her experience.

It is clear, however, that Julian also read and wrote in the vernacular and could probably read Latin and she knew a number of important theologians including Augustine, Gregory the Great and William of St. Thierry and possibly the Rhineland mystics, like Meister Eckhart and John Tauler. Norwich was a flourishing center of scholarship at the time she was writing, including a Benedictine priory with a magnificent library. It is also interesting to note that John Wycliff was vigorously promoting the Bible in the vernacular and the first complete translation was in 1390, during Julian's lifetime. Even though this carried with it the odor of heresy, Julian decided that she too would write in her native tongue, so that it would be available to her fellow-Christians.

It is impossible to know when Julian was shut up in her anchor-hold. The vocation of an anchoress was one in which people of the middle ages would have been much more familiar with than we are today. This was the lifestyle of the early desert fathers and mothers and reflected the impulse toward austerity and solitary living. This opened up the space for prayer, reflection and silence which allowed one to deepen one's intercourse with God. Anchor-holds within a city like Norwich were usually one room, attached to a church, where the anchoress would be shut in for the rest of her life. There were windows: one which opened into the church for the viewing of the Mass, and one onto the street to converse with visitors. In this way, her vows enabled her to offer counsel to those seeking spiritual direction and yet still live a solitary life similar to a monastic.

In her counseling of others, at least in the reflections that emerge from her writing, she wishes to place more emphasis on the reality of God in people's experience rather than in the theory of God. For Julian, God's actions are motivated by love for humanity. She wants to focus on the way God's love can be manifest in the midst of suffering because it is through love that individual salvation happens. Her emphasis on God's love and mercy and her acknowledgment that there is much beyond human knowing is perhaps why there is a notable absence of hell in her writings.

One form that Julian's theology takes is, like the Savior whom she loves so dearly, the metaphor or parable. An often quoted one is the parable of the master and the servant. Yet she writes about this parable as if it were shown to her in a vision. In it she sees the master of a large estate seated on a throne and a poorly dressed servant arrives to attend him. The master sends him off to do a task and he happily departs. In his great haste, he falls into a ditch and is injured; he cannot get out of his predicament and is suffering greatly. In addition to his physical pain, he experiences deep loneliness and spiritual suffering, including blindness of reason, which means that he even forgets the love of his master. In the parable, it is obvious that, for Julian, spiritual suffering is about separation from God. The servant not only experiences pain and fear but also doubt and faithlessness and its consequent dread. In the parable, the servant suffers while being unable to turn his head; if he could do so he would see that his beloved Lord is nearby. He has great love and compassion for his servant and is on the way to rescue him. The master says, "See my beloved servant, what harm and injury he has taken in my service and for my love, and yes, for his good will; is it not reasonable that I should reward him his fright and his fear?" So, like the Job story, the servant is rescued and doubly rewarded.

And in this, as in so much of Julian's theology, in the end "all shall be well and all manner of thing shall be well." Julian has a strong view of Divine Providence; for what is apparent if one reads her closely is that, no matter what may happen, the entire creation is in God's hands and has been since before the beginning, for "before God made us he loved us, and this love has never abated, and never shall be." Of this, Julian seems certain.

How did Julian's theology evolve? When she was a girl, Julian tells us, she initially prayed for three things, which she kept in her heart for many years. First, she asked for an understanding of Christ's passion—and not merely an intellectual one. She wanted to participate in it, like his mother or Mary Magdelene who stood at his feet when he died. Second, she asked for an illness that would bring her close to death, so that she may understand that part of Christ's passion, and third she asked for three "wounds." She wanted true contrition, loving compassion, and a complete longing for God's will alone. Julian initially forgot about her first two wishes, until the time of her deathly illness, but she continued to pray for the three attributes that she felt would bring her closer to God.

Then, when she was 30 years old, one of her prayers was mysteriously answered and she became seriously ill and nearly died. Those around her sent for a priest to give her last rites. It is unclear what the illness was, for Julian does not dwell on it except to say that her whole body went numb and her vision seemed to have disappeared except for a small circle of light. A cross was held before her and although everything else in the room was black, she fixed her eyes on the crucifix. At one point, when she felt she was indeed dying, she had a kind of 'temptation' to look heavenward in search of God waiting for her there; yet something restrained her from moving her eyes from the cross.

During this time she had an intense vision of the bleeding face of Christ, including a sorrowful look at his mother, Mary, the pain of which Julian felt keenly.

Then, in the midst of this suffering, she saw a change in Christ and his appearance became very joyful. He then conversed with her about many things which she later wrote about. She seemed to have a number of spiritual illuminations at this time, including the often-quoted hazel nut revelation, which would form the basis of her theology of creation.

Julian's experience was therefore composed of her bodily experience which she saw with her eyes (the crucifix bleeding); her locutions or conversation, which she remembered in detail after her recovery; and a set of spiritual visions or insights which she clearly distinguished from the bodily vision. Meditation on the suffering of Christ was a popular visualization technique during this period and also reflected the Pauline theology of Phil. 3: 10-11: "that I may know him and the power of resurrection and may share in his sufferings, becoming like him in death that if possible I may attain the resurrection from the dead" and also Mat. 16:24, to take up one's cross and follow Christ. Various Biblical visualizations would have likely been incorporated into the meditative technique of the Rosary.

It should be noted that her first wish, then—to enter into Christ's passion—was not an unusual one during the middle ages; many for instance, asked for the stigmata or for the ability to suffer as Christ suffered. But this was not Julian's desire. She wanted to stand at the foot of the cross as a perfect disciple. And although Julian's request to develop an empathy for Christ's passion, to increase her love and devotion to him, was not an unusual desire, her second request—to undergo a severe illness to manifest the recollection of his death—demonstrates the seriousness of her purpose. Julian was aware that this identification with Christ would also include an identification with those for whom he suffered. Participation in the suffering of Christ implies, for Julian, a continuing process of holding on at all cost, and in the culture in which she lived it would imply that nobody gets by unscathed. After two waves of the Black Death in her town everyone would have known someone who had died. In her later counseling Julian would no doubt have emphasized that it is only at the foot of the cross that an inner coherence emerges. Suffering is a mystery and a means for grace in Julian's theology, where the one thing we can hold onto is the certainty that God's grace and mercy will never abandon us.

Julian's theology does not reflect the prevailing penitential system of the early middle ages that viewed sin as an offense against God who demanded penance adequate for particular sins. This is evident in her parable of the fallen servant. Rather, she developed an understanding which moved away from external forms of contrition toward an internal compunction for sin coupled with acceptance of divine mercy. In this, she prefigures a Reformation theology: unless the grace of God penetrates the heart, any form of reparation for sin was well beyond human capability. She reflects on how human brokenness is met by the healing love of God.

The wound of loving compassion which Julian had asked of Christ demonstrates the depth of sharing in Christ's pity for the sinner, whom he wished not to rebuke but rather to heal. This compassion would undoubtedly have made her a sensitive listener as she counseled the many troubled souls who found their way to her window.

Although Julian's feast day is celebrated in in the Roman Catholic tradition on May 13, she was never officially sainted. This could be due to her theology, (sometimes called apokatastasis, or universal salvation) laid down in her final *Long Text* where she said, "Here I was taught by the grace of God that I should steadfastly keep in the faith... and that at the same time I should take my stand on and earnestly believe in what our Lord showed in this time—that there is a secret to be revealed at the time of judgment—that 'all manner of thing shall be well.'"

Julian's feast day is also kept in the Anglican and Lutheran traditions, and the Episcopal Church has a religious order named after her: The Order of Julian of Norwich, composed of enclosed monks and nuns, with oblates and associates across the United States.

Part 2:

Julian's Theology on Creation, the Trinity, and the Nature of the Soul

Julian's Theology of Creation

"We were all created at the same time. And in our creation, we were all knit and oned to God."

The real value of the Revleations of Julian of Norwich, which she has called her "Showings" does not lie in the vision or exact locutions themselves, but in the fact that a Transcendent God animates Julian's experience, creating an intimate contact that she wishes to share with us, her "even-Christians" (or fellow Christians). Often a visionary or mystic is graced by an infusion of wisdom and spiritual insight that takes form in symbols. The symbolic images we would like to explore from Julian's Showings are the hazel-nut vision, the image of God as Trinity, and the parable of the fallen servant. Through these, we uncover Julian's theology of creation, her understanding of the motherhood of God, and her theodicy.

In one of her showings described in chapter 11, Julian perceives, in some way, God in a single *point*: "After this, I saw God in a point, that is to say, in my understanding, and in this sight I saw that he is in all things..." This led her to the understanding of this locution: "Look, I am God. I am in all...I never cease upholding my work and I never will. I am guiding everything toward the end I ordained for it from the first..." Julian's *God in a point* epiphany enables her to experience not only that God is, but that God is the ground of everything that is. God is nearer to us than our own soul and therefore God leads everything to the ultimate end for which it was created. Julian is hearing the Spirit within her mind describe the world as it is forever being created by perfect Wisdom, "where all is as it was created to be." We will return to this image of Wisdom momentarily.

Julian's hazel-nut vision was similar to her beholding of God in a point. Hazelnuts were so utterly ordinary in that part of England that it was something of an epiphany that it suddenly became an entire cosmos. For her understanding was that, "It is *all* that is made," yet it still seemed so terribly small and inconsequential that it could well disintegrate into nothingness.

And yet, through her inner eye, like a telescope, zooming out into infinite space, she saw it suspended and held by God's unseen hand, like the image of the earth itself, floating in space. And God assures her that it will last because God loves it, and in the same way "do all things exist or have their being" from one second to the next, solely because of the love of God. Julian seems to see all of creation, in fact, in this symbol. And precisely because God loves it, it ceases to be inconsequential or ordinary.

Julian is here given a glimpse of what many other mystics have claimed to have seen: that creation is nothing else but the expression of Divine Love. Her understanding about the hazel-nut vision is that first, "God has made it"; second, that "God loves it" and third, "God protects it." This reflects a Trinitarian understanding, as she expresses it in the Short Text, "where God is truly the lover, the maker, and the keeper."

At the same time, Julian sees the "nothingness" of the entire creation as reflecting this: that "created things are nothing, and we must turn aside from them to love and have our God who is not made." (Chapter 5) This leads her to compose the prayer that every member of the Julian Order murmurs in her heart at the end of every day, "God, of your goodness, give me yourself; for you are enough to me. And may I ask nothing less that may be full worship to you. And if I ask anything less, I am ever left wanting; But only in you have I all." (Chapter 5) In a later showing, Julian sees that even more than the entire creation, God rejoices at the creation of a human being's soul, "for It (the Trinity) saw without beginning what would delight It without end." (Chapter 68)

When Julian sees that God is "guiding everything toward the end I ordained" (Chapter 5) and later when she also understands that "God never changed his purpose in any kind of thing" (Chapter 11) Julian is penetrating momentarily into the order and purpose of God, where she saw that everything is done "by God's prescient wisdom." This is firmly rooted in the Wisdom tradition, where the female principle of Wisdom was "a pure emanation of the glory of the Almighty" (Wis. 7: 25-26); and it was by Wisdom that the earth was formed (Prov. 3: 19). Following in the Wisdom tradition, St. Paul wrote that Christ is the "Wisdom of God." (1 Cor. 1: 24) Although some of the earlier Syrian and Greek Fathers associated the Wisdom figure with the Holy Spirit, in most of the Latin Fathers, through numerous theologians of the 12th century (e.g., St. Bernard) the analogy of Christ as Wisdom was popular. This was the Person who was actively present at the creation of the universe, rejoicing and delighting with Yahweh (Prov. 8: 22-31) and in whose image humanity is created for eternal life with God.

Julian's view of human creation in and through Christ is apparent in the showings where she sees that all of humanity was created "all at once," when God prepared a human nature for the 2nd Person of the Trinity. All human nature was united to God's Wisdom in that instant and Julian sees in it, "the noblest thing which God has ever made." (Chapter 53) Julian seems to imply here that the whole human race is the full human nature of Christ. What's more, "we are God's creation twice: essential being and sensual substance"; that is, through Christ, "in whom we are founded and rooted." (Chapters 56, 58)

In this understanding of the union of spirit with matter, soul and body, Julian is most probably reflecting the influence of Christian Neoplatonism, wherein the second Person of the Trinity, the Logos, is both the thought and word of God. Since Christ is the true image of God, humanity is the true image of Christ. Following the Neoplatonists of the Greek fathers and Augustine, God creates humans in the divine image and likeness through the agency of the second Person, the uncreated image of God, who is the Father's created

Word impressing form upon matter. In Julian's understanding—and this belongs more to the Greek Orthodox tradition than to the Roman tradition— the 'likeness' is what makes a human person whole, holy and capable of being divinized. It is also this 'likeness' that can be stained and lost to sin, as in the parable of the fallen servant, which we will revisit in a later section.

However, in Chapter 10, Julian says, "We know in our faith and in our belief...that the blessed Trinity made humankind *to his image and to his likeness*" (Gen 1: 26-27). In Greek Orthodox theology, the 'image' of God in the soul can never be erased, even though the likeness can be tarnished. In Julian's seeing, the spiritual powers of the soul (reason, memory and will) are given to us and are therefore 'godly.' In Chapter 53 Julian explains that at the creation, human beings are intertwined into an existential union with God which is beyond the will of any person to deny or destroy. Yet because of our strong tendency to misuse our soul's powers, she understands that Christ's redemption was necessary to liberate us from the distorting influence of evil. Thus the Incarnation, which is Gods merciful work in time, completes human nature. In Julian's theology, (and there is an evolutionary perspective here, as in the work of numerous modern theologians) the assumption of the human likeness (the sensuality) with the divine image (or its essence or substance) happens by a gradual progress of growth in the life of grace, ("until we have grown to full stature as creative nature brings about") through the presence of the Holy Spirit. "And then, in the foundation of creative nature with the operation of mercy, the Holy Spirit by grace breathes into us gifts leading to endless life." (Chapter 55)

Although the body is made of elements ("the slime of the earth") and—as we know now—evolved over time, Julian sees the soul as "made of nothing...and thus is the created nature rightly united to the maker who is essential nature and uncreated; in other words, God. From which it follows there can lie nothing at all between God and man's soul." (Chapter 53) Julian here seems to intuit that the soul's nature itself is the *image* of God and that it rests in sensuality while embodied. Julian diverges significantly from the Augustinian tradition by refusing to restrict the image of God to the higher reason; instead, she asserts that it also informs the sensuality, and both belong to the soul.

Julian's Theology of the Trinity

"And thus…almighty God is our natural Father and God, all wisdom, is our natural Mother, with the love and goodness of the Holy Spirit, who is all one God."

In chapter 1 Julian gives us a hint that the Trinity will form an important part of her theology, and a Trinitarian focus is laced throughout her work. She takes up the theme of the Trinity in chapter 22 when she says the three great joys of heaven are co-related to the Persons of the Trinity. The Father's revelation is his nature and mode of working; that of the Logos is the joy of redemption; and the Spirit is eternal delight. Julian exalts the soul's great capacity to be able to contemplate truth in the Father, wisdom in the Son, and love through the delight of the Spirit.

She sees the soul as a creature in God which mirrors the divine Trinity, because it is made in its image. In chapter 44 she talks about the immense dignity given to it by virtue of the clarity and purity of understanding granted to a creature so low compared to a Creator "so high, so great and so good." In chapter 32 Julian is reflecting on the sorrow and mournfulness of humanity which she must have perceived often passing by her window. Our depressed state can even interfere with our ability to relax into "the blessed contemplation of God as we ought." She believes that our reasoning minds become "blind, low and simple" because we cannot really comprehend the transcendence of the Trinity in it's glorious might, wisdom and goodness. This is why, for Julian, we must rest on the words of Christ that all will be well, for only in this lies our salvation. She affirms that the whole Trinity worked in the passion of Christ, but "only the Virgin's Son suffered." (chapter 23) Like a mother whose body gives a material nature to her unborn child, Christ also substantially gives birth to humanity.

Although there were numerous predecessors to Julian in seeing mother attributes in God, for example, St. Bernard, Albert the Great, Hildegard, and Bonaventure, it is unclear if Julian knew their writings. What is clear is that Julian does not treat God's Motherhood merely as a metaphor for divine kindness, wisdom, compassion, or justice. Nor does she speak of God's maternity as a simile, inferring that Christ is 'like' an earthly mother. Rather, she appears to think of the Motherhood of the second Person of the Trinity as equal to the Fatherhood of God in the first Person. Existentially, God is our Mother as well as our Father.

In the same way, Julian reifies Christ as our Spouse. By the "knitting and oneing to humanity" the Incarnation becomes both our closest lover and our dearest Mother. It is something of a theological risk to stretch the analogy for motherhood or spousal beloved in this way but it seems like a part of her Revelation, not just her informed theology. Her revelations, or showings are very personal, and also connected to the sacraments.

"our beloved Mother, Jesus, feeds us with himself and with the most tender courtesy, does it by means of the Blessed Sacrament."

For Julian, where Christ is, there is Trinity, unity, and the highest good in everything. Julian sees that the soul's substantial being, which is so noble and honorable, is also extremely meek and mild before the mystery of the union of Christ's divine and human natures. Her use of motherhood to describe Christ is revealed in chapter 60 when she explains how we are brought back into our pristine natural state "by the motherhood of mercy and grace." Christ, as Savior, brings us "back" because through his grace we are restored to "that natural condition which was ours originally when we were made through the motherhood of natural love, which has never left us."

Because a mother's role is the "most intimate, willing and truest of all" only Christ can properly fulfill it. Earthly mothers bear us into a world of both joy and pain, but Christ "bears us to joy and eternal life. Thus he carries us within himself in love." (Chapter 60) And not until "when this is over and we ourselves have been born to eternal bliss, is his marvelous love completely satisfied."

Another reason Julian reifies the concept of the motherhood of Christ is because of the Sacrament of the Eucharist, as we saw in the above quote about feeding. Julian sees the Eucharist as completely nurturing. As a baby is literally kept alive by its mother's milk, so our Mother Christ gives us his own body and blood, which prior to the Reformation, of course, was not just a symbol. The Eucharist was the ritual of becoming one with the mystical body of Christ, and is closely tied to Christ taking on our human nature: "the second Person of the Trinity is our mother in nature in our substantial making...and he is our mother of mercy by taking our sensuality."

In her showing about the motherhood, she also utilizes a common image that even found its way onto the cover of missals or prayer-books of the time. "He leads us into his blessed breast by his sweet open side." (Chapter 60) In other words, the pierced side of Christ is not only the wound by which his life-saving blood flows, but for Julian, it becomes the entrance into the "joys of heaven and the certainty of endless bliss." In this showing, Julian saw Christ looking at the wound in his open side and saying, "lo, how I love thee." Christ communicates his own spiritual thirst to those who belong to his body and therefore Christ's lovers are caught up in the desire of Christ and share in his compassion.

After these startling images in chapter 60, Julian turns to the ways Christ brings us forth spiritually. She calls this a "ghostly forth-bringing." Through this "he makes us love whatever he loves for love of him." It is here that Julian reaches the understanding that "it is his business to save us; it is his glory to do this for us; and it is his will that we know it." It is at this time that Julian experiences the most complete spiritual nourishment during her Revelations, for she feels Christ at work in every aspect of her coming to understand the hidden meanings of her previous visions and locutions. At the end of this showing, she hears Christ say, "I will keep you safe and sound."

"To the property of motherhood belong nature, love, wisdom, and knowledge; and this is God." (Chapter 60) This is perhaps why her contemplative understanding is that none should be lost for, although Christ as Mother may "sometimes suffer the child to fall" he can "never suffer us who are his children to perish." (Chapter 61)

In a time when women's bodies were generally perceived as nature's foiled attempt at creating a male—that is, when women were often characterized as inherently degraded and inferior, particularly because they are daughters of Eve and a source of temptation to the more exalted sex, it is all the more astonishing that Julian's showings uncovered such a feminine and tender savior in Christ.

It should be noted that, as Julian is able to image Christ's motherhood, she sees the sex of Jesus as clearly male. Julian nowhere hints that what she is seeing is an androgynous or feminine figure. When Julian sees Christ, she sees, "Lord Jesus, true God and true man, a handsome person and tall...his face was lovely pale brown with a very seemly countenance, his eyes were black, most beautiful and seemly." (Chapters 68 and 51) However, she would have certainly been aware of the Latin Vulgate, which included all of the Wisdom books, now considered apocryphal in King James and later Protestant Bibles. She would have no doubt known Sirach, where the partner with God says "I am the mother of fair love" (Sirach 24:24) as well as the Wisdom text that associates the feminine Sophia (Wisdom) with the Savior: "People learn what pleases you and are saved by Sophia." (Wisdom 9:18) Julian knew the Wisdom books. And she also knew Augustine.

It is this characterization—the divine motherhood— where Julian separates herself from Augustine's anthropology. This was explained in part in our earlier section on Julian's theology of creation, where "our image and likeness" are enclosed in God since the beginning, because Christ has taken on our human nature. "He is the means which keeps the substance and the sensuality together, so that they will never separate." (Chaper 55) Here Julian corrects Augustine's view in which the human being takes only matter from the mother. For Augustine, the image of God was the rational soul; a woman's body, which operates from the feminine part of the soul, is therefore not an image of God.

Furthermore, this was precisely the place where Augustine sees original sin as having roots in sexual concupscience—as well as in the womb of the mother. In the first chapter of his *Confession*, he asks God: "if I was 'conceived in iniquity and in sin did my mother nourish me within her womb' (quoting Psalm 51), where, O Lord, or when was I—your servant—ever innocent?" For Augustine, Adam of course is the transmitter of original sin through his active seed, for which the woman is the passive receptor. But the sin really came from the temptation of Eve.

It could be noted in this respect that Augustine's (and the resulting Latin) theory of original sin is not the Greek Orthodox understanding (eg., it is not found in Athanasius or Gregory of Nyssa). In fact, Orthodoxy never canonized Augustine because of his faulty theology about original sin. But Julian—herself theologizing only from her images—also turns the tables on Augustinian anthropology when she speaks of Jesus as a mother who "can lead us easily into his breast through his open side, and show us there a part of the Godhead." (Chapter 60)

Perhaps the most important point here is that Julian confirms the goodness of our human nature through the motherhood of Jesus: eg., "in his taking of our nature, where the motherhood of grace begins."   (Chapter 59) In her *Models of God,* Sallie McFague has noted that, unlike all other medieval attributions of maternal imagery in God, Julian alone understands Christ as "substantially" and not just "accidentally" affirming the feminine nature. "We owe our being to him, and this is the essence of motherhood." (Chapter 59)

Julian, extremely simply and covertly, corrects Augustine's vision of humanity as ineluctably dual; rather, she glorifies the duality of human spirit and physicality. And, as we will see when we examine Julian's theodicy, because Christ is the New Adam, our sensuality is thereby redeemed.

Julian's Trinity reflects an Eastern Orthodox theology much more than a Latin one, a point which has been made by numerous Orthodox writers, who see in Julian a saint "after their own Orthodox heart." It has been theorized that perhaps Julian knew pseudo-Dionysius or even Maximus, (6th cent.) but this cannot be reliably demonstrated. However, in both Orthodox mysticism and Julian's showings, the dynamic *indwelling* of the Persons of the Trinity is what constitutes personhood in God. That is, God is personal because of the intimate interactions of the Trinitarian relationships. In this, Julian's theology recapitulates an Orthodox concept known as *perichoresis*.

This term refers to the indwelling of the Father "in" the Son, the Son "in" the Spirit, the Spirit "in" the Father, and so on. This is at the heart of the mystery in which the whole of each Person actively lives in the whole of the others. In addition, all that has being participates in God's being, thus God is the "true Father and true Mother of natures." (Chapter 62)

The tendency in the West (since Augustine) of depicting the Holy Spirit as the "love-bond" between the Father and the Son is never found in the East, which feels this is a rather reductive approach to the personhood of the Holy Spirit. Julian also avoids the tendency to view divine love as the peculair action of the Holy Spirit, but rather identifies Love as Being and therefore with the interaction of all of the Persons with each other and with humanity.

In the incarnational *perichoresis*, the Logos is located "in" humanity and also "in" the Persons and that is how humanity becomes permanently located "in" God, a process known as deification. The love that Julian perceives in the Trinity is developed in one of her last showings thus:
"I had three kinds of understanding of this love: love that is uncreated, love that is created, and love that is given. Uncreated love is God; created love Is our soul

31

in God; and love that is given is charity or virtue. It is a gracious gift and it works in us so that we love God for himself, and love ourselves in God; and love what God loves, for his sake." (Chapter 84)

For Julian, the whole Trinity, not just the Father, is the Creator, and thus "dwells eternally in our soul in Christ Jesus our Savior." (Chapter 1) Through grace and sanctification, humans participate in this inner life of all the Persons. Christ leads us to "his city in rest and peace, which the Father has prepared." Here, the Trinity is described in multiple triads, which should not, however, be seen as separate attributes. Julian's favorite descriptions are truth, wisdom, charity; joy, bliss and delight; and nature, mercy, and grace. For example, the gift of humanity which Christ presents to the Father "is joy to the Father, and bliss to the Son, and delight to the Holy Spirit."

Similar to the divinization process set in motion by virtue of Christ's incarnation ("God became human so that humans may become divine" said Athanasius), Julian sees humanity mirroring the Trinity: "For God is endless truth, endless supreme wisdom, endless supreme love uncreated, and the human soul is a creature in God which has the same properties created." (Chapter 44)

Julian's Theodicy

Julian understands the nature of Christ's divine mercy and his promise that all will be well within the context and scope of God's salvific activity; however, she also knows this has the potential to conflict with the official teaching and the popular piety of the medieval church. At times in her writing, Julian's anxiety indicates that this conflict might force her to choose between the official church teaching and the showings in her revelations, and if this were so, it may indeed place her outside of the boundaries of the body of Christ. Julian was well aware that a woman teacher or preacher was not welcome in the church during the period in which she lived. Women did not have priestly functions because they did not represent the image of God. She would have known Augustine's assessment of Eve:
"When she is assigned as a help-mate, a function that pertains to her alone, then she is not the image of God, but as far as man is concerned, he is by himself alone the image of God." *(de Trinitate)* But she also would have been aware of Paul's injunction that in Christ "there is neither male nor female" (Gal. 3: 28) and that, since all are God's children, we are all co-heirs in Christ. (Rom. 8:17)

Julian, alone in her cell for much of her life, ruminated often on her reveleations, and her theology is a direct outgrowth from them. The teaching of the lord and the servant, recounted in the first section on Julian's life in context, is one which she meditated on for many years. Initially, she sees that because the lord is always with the fallen servant, even though he was unaware of it, that Christ not only does not blame the fallen servant, but blesses him in his fallenness. And Christ seems to say to her that "it is my wish that you know this," that is, "that I shall make good all the wrongs of whatever degree." (Chapter 29)

In this showing, Christ seemed to indicate that "the glorious reparation" which he accomplished was more "pleasing and honorable to God than ever was the sin of Adam," and presumably Adam's descendants. This is because Julian sees Adam, not as a historical figure, but (like Paul) an archetype representing humanity. But this seems to contradict the church's teaching on damnation, and Julian is quick to say "in all things I believe as holy church teaches." (Chapter 9) At the same time, she must believe her showings, and they reveal nothing of the damned. The fact that for a long time she could not reconcile this conflict was troubling, and she wrote, "as to this I had no other answer revealed by our Lord except this: 'what is impossible to you is not impossible to me. I will honor my word in every respect.'" (Chapter 32)

Still Julian remains confused and unconvinced and says that she desired to see hell and purgatory, since the church taught this as doctrine. She must have been aware that other visionaries did have such visions. Yet, she says she "could see nothing of this." (Chapter 33) She is so troubled by her *lack* of vision she wonders if there was some defect in her revelation. And eventually she comes to accept that this "great deed eternally ordained by God [is] treasured and hidden in his blessed breast, known only to him," but there was indeed "a great secret...that the most blessed Trinity will do on the last day" and the way this will manifest is "unknown by any creature beneath Christ." (Chapter 32)

The boundaries of the elect group (of the saved) seem to continually stretch to include all of humanity and ultimately, the whole creation. In her theology she seems to see that the *spiritual* thirst of Christ on the cross is his desire for Adam (humanity) and nothing less than Adam's full redemption will slake that thirst.

It is Christ's love that binds all of humanity together, as one in the mystical body, and this is, in fact, what salvation is: ie., participation in the divine life. "God will make us all to be at one with him." (Chapter 71) Because of the universal nature of Adam and because Christ, as the second Adam, subsumed all of creation into his mystical body, we are all connected:
"The love of God makes us into such a unity that when it is truly seen, no person can separate themselves from another." (Chapter 65)

God's will is to save humanity and that will is grounded in divine Love. The body of the archetypal Adam is one that can be whole only in the transgression of its boundaries, and this happens through the infinite mercy of God displayed at the crucifixion of Christ. Julian, in her deathbed experience, refused to take her eyes off of the cross, and she understood that it is in the crucified humanity of Jesus that all contradictions are ultimately reconciled. This is the Event, which for Julian encompasses the extremes of circumference and center, abolishing all boundaries. It is an image whose contours are expanded into infinity and in this way enfolds all possible oppositions.

In one of her showings, God seemed to draw her into the crucified Word of God, which indeed seems beyond human understanding. This is the "foolishness of God embodied." In the image she beheld of the continually and profusely bleeding body of Jesus, Julian saw a body that could not contain its boundaries, a body that renders itself passive to the forces acting upon it. As she sees it, the body of Jesus has no specific territory that it must protect because its interior has been exteriorized through his sacrifice.

Julian's great revelation, after meditating on the showing of the fallen servant for many years, is that the servant is not only an image of fallen Adam, it is also an image of *Christ:* The redemption of humanity involves Christ coming to dwell in our sensuality. She heard Christ say, "See my dear Father, I stand before you in Adam's tunic." The servant who struggles and suffers in the ditch is also the body of Jesus in the process of the reconciliation of his essence with our sensuality. She suddenly saw that "When Adam fell, God's Son fell." (Chapter 51) This is the spiritual meaning behind the 'literal' meaning and therefore "we have in us the wretchedness and misfortune of Adam's falling," but we also have "in us our Lord Jesus Christ resurrected." (Chapter 52)

In the suffering servant, who is then united with the new Adam, Christ, the image of God is restored. As a result, the wisdom of the human soul which originally mirrored Divine Wisdom and became obscured is also restored, as Christ is our perfect Wisdom. Faith enables the restoration and increase of wisdom and might and this "works great things in us for Christ is mercifully working in us." (Chapter 54)

The difference between the "falling" of the servant-Adam and the servant-Christ is that Christ was not an unwilling sacrifice; he willing parcipates in our suffering (by "wearing Adam's tunic"). The servant unwillingly and unwittingly falls, but Christ's act of lowering himself to humanity's needs by assuming the human condition is done out of love. Julian's theology does not seem to have room for the theory of justification. The atonement is really an at-one-ment. And it is clear that, for Julian, Adam represents all of humanity, the "social body" of Christ, and in this sense, she sees this suffering body in the society all around her. This too is the body of one who is persecuted, and like the open wound of Christ, invites her to continually enter through her compassionate listening and understanding. This is where the literal and allegorical interpretations of the "fall" really merge.

That Julian revises the interpretation of the Fall in the Genesis story is a bold theology in which all human beings, male and female, represent the image of God in both body and soul. Julian never mentions Eve in the Gensis story, although she often uses the word Adam. It is apparent in her theology that Adam and Christ transcend their 'maleness' and represent the whole of humanity. This is in complete accordance with the Chalcedonian formula which emphasizes Christ's humanness, not his maleness; because the historical maleness of Jesus was not "essential"; rather it was "assumed." In this sense, Julian's Christology could never be seen as a "Christology from below." Even with the stress on Christ's suffering humanness he is never considered apart from his identity as the second Person of the Trinity.

For Julian, the divine nature is imprinted upon the world in the Trinitarian exchange of gifts. The Father is the origin of the Son's gift of being human, and the Son, as the Servant, is predestined from all eternity to bring the gift of himself to the Father as the new Adam. The whole human race is engrafted onto this gift exchange between the Son and the Father, "for I saw that Christ, having all of us within him...honorably presents his Father in heaven with us, and this gift his Father thankfully receives..." (Chapter 55)

We have seen that the "thirst" which Christ experienced on the cross became in her understanding the spiritual thirst for souls which was his motivation to assume a human body: he ardently longed to participate in the human passion; and he told Julian he would have suffered more of it if it would have been possible. (Chapter 24) What's more, this passionate longing is not yet at an end. "It persists and always will until we see him on the day of judgment... his thirst is...to gather us all into himself." (Chapter 31)

This, then, is how Julian describes Christ's 'fall' in the parable of the suffering servant:

"So he stood before his Father as a servant, deliberately, making himself responsible for us. He started off with all eagerness at his Father's will and at once he fell into the Virgin's womb, regardless of himself or his cruel pains." (Chapter 51) This echoes Paul (in Phil. 2:5-11) when he speaks about the 'kenosis' of Christ; he "did not count equality with God a thing to be grasped, but emptied himself taking the form of a servant..."

When the servant is thus transformed his work becomes not only reparation but renewal: this is the work of the new creation. This can only happen because Christ's substance is nature's substance. This is also why Julian's theology of creation is not dualistic; this is not a tainted world, it is rather, a creation of goodness:

"From this substantial nature spring mercy and grace and penetrate us, accomplishing everything for the fulfillment of our great joy." (Chapter 56)

As in Rom. 8: 17, we (Adam) share in Christ's suffering but we also will be glorified with him in the resurrection. The two servants merge, as cross and resurrection are inextricably linked in Julian's initial vision, where she chose to focus her whole conscious being:

"No other heaven was pleasing to me than Jesus...ever since, this has been a great comfort to me, that by his grace I chose him, in all his passion and grief." (Chapter 19)

This work of salvation is continually going on for:
"Our God, Mother Jesus, in accepting our nature, quickened us to life, and in his blessed dying on the cross, he bore us to endless life." (Chapter 63)

Meanwhile, "he carries us within him in love and travail" much like a woman in labor.

Thus Julian's theodicy is very positive. Although humanity experiences itself as alienated from God and from one another, this in no way is attributed to the wrath of God or even to our disobedience. We learn from Julian that meditation on the life, passion and death of Christ instills the gift of grace and with it great hope. And that hope is that we will be brought into final union with God in the eternal bliss of Jesus:
"We are his bliss, we are his reward, we are his honor, and we are his crown. And this was a singular wonder and a most delectable contemplation."

Selected Meditations

Truth sees God, wisdom beholds God and from these two comes a third, a holy wondering delight in God, which is love. Where there is truth and wisdom there also is true love, springing from them both.

When we die we shall come to God knowing ourselves clearly, having God wholly. We shall be enfolded in God forever, seeing him truly, feeling him fully, hearing him spiritually, smelling him delectably, and tasting him sweetly.

Our Lord gave me a spiritual revelation of his homely loving. I saw that he is everything to us that is good. He is our clothing. His love envelops and embraces and encloses us. Because of his tender love He hovers about us and will never leave us.

God wills to be known and it pleases him that we find our rest in him. For nothing that is beneath him satisfies us. And this is the reason why no soul will find rest until it is set free from all that is made. When a person is completely emptied, through love, in order to have him who is all that is good, then [s]he is able to receive spiritual rest.

He showed me a little thing the size of a hazelnut lying in the palm of my hand, and it seemed to me to be as round as a ball. I looked at it and thought, 'What can this be?' and I was answered thus: 'It is all that is made.' I marveled how it could last, because it seemed to me that it might fall suddenly to pieces because of its littleness. And I was answered in my understanding, 'It lasts and always will because God loves it. And in the same way, everything has its being through the love of God.'

Every natural feeling of compassion that a person feels for his fellow humans is because Christ is in him. When contrition fills a person through the activity of the Holy Spirit, then bitterness is turned to hope in God's mercy.

Our good Lord answered all questions and doubts with comfort; 'I will make all things well. I may make all things well and I can make all things well, and you yourself will see that all manner of things shall be well.'

God is the point of stillness at the Center. He is the
Ground. He is the Essence. He is the Teaching. He is
the Teacher. He is the End. He is the center for which
every true person strives, and he is known and shall be
known to every person to whom the Holy Spirit reveals
him. Our Lord Jesus said,
"It is I who am highest,
it is I whom you love,
it is I whom you delight in,
it is I whom you serve.
it is I whom you long for,
it is I whom you desire,
it is I whom you contemplate;
It is I who am all."

Prayer unites the soul to God. Prayer makes harmony between God and a person's soul. But when a person is close to God he has no need to pray, but reverently meditates on what God says. At the time this was shown to me, I was not moved to pray, but had this well of comfort in my mind--that when we see God, we have what we desire, and prayer is unnecessary. But when God is hidden from us, then we must pray to prepare ourselves for Jesus.

And therefore we may with his grace and his help continue to see things from a spiritual perspective while marvelling endlessly at this high, over-passing, immeasurable love that almighty God has for us in his goodness. And therefore we may ask from our lover with reverence all that we wish, for our natural will is to have God and the good will of God is to have us. And we may never cease willing or longing until we have him in fullness of joy, and then we will not be able to will anything more, for he wills that we be engaged in knowing and loving until the time when we shall find fulfillment in heaven.

At this same time our Lord showed me a spiritual vision of how warmly and intimately he loves. I saw that he is to us everything that is good and comforting for us. He is our clothing which, for love, wraps and embraces us and, from his tender love, completely encloses us so that he may never leave us. And so in this showing, I saw that he is everything to us that is good, as I understood it.

We were all created at the same time. And in our creation, we were all knit and oned to God. By this, we are kept as luminous and noble as when we were created. By the force of this precious oneing, we love, seek, praise, thank, and endlessly enjoy our Creator.

Our lover desires that our soul should cling to him with all its might, and that we should ever hold fast to his goodness. For this above all else pleases God and strengthens the soul.

I saw and I understood that our faith is our light in darkness, and this light is God, our endless day. The light is charity, and this light is given to us by God's wisdom, according to our need. For the light is not so great that we see the blessed day of heaven now; nor is it denied us. But we are given enough light to live profitably, with labor, deserving the endless glory of God.

And I understood the reverent way in which she [Mary] gazed at her God and maker, marvelling with great reverence that he wished to be born of her who was a simple creature whom he had made. And this wisdom and truth, this knowing of the greatness of her maker and the littleness of herself who had been created made her say full meekly to Gabriel, "Behold me, the handmaid of the Lord."

Lord, you know what I want if it be your will that I have it; and if it be not your will, good Lord, be not displeased, for I want nothing which you do not want.

I now saw that our Lord rejoices in the tribulations of his servants with pity and compassion; and to each person whom he loves he lays on them something which carries no blame in his sight, although it causes them to be blamed in this world, despised, or scorned or mocked. This he does to forestall the harm they might have from the pomps and the pride and the empty glories of this life, and to prepare their way to come to heaven and to exalt them in everlasting bliss. For he says..."I shall enclose you and, by uniting myself to you, make you humble and mild, pure and holy."

This is the cause we are not at rest in heart and soul: that here we seek rest in things in things that are so little there is no rest in them...When the soul gives up all for love, so that it can have him who is all, then it finds true rest. For he is endless and has made us for his own self, and has restored us by his blessed passion, and keeps us in his blessed love. And he does all this through his goodness.

Under his watchfulness we fall; by his blessed love and strength and wisdom we are defended; and through mercy and through grace we are lifted up to many joys.

And so I saw surely that before God ever made us, he loved us. And this love was never quenched nor ever shall be....and in this love he has made everything profitable for us, and in this love, our life is everlasting. In our making we had a beginning, but the love in which he made us was in him from the beginning, in which love we have our beginning.

Light is the origin of life; night the origin of pain and grief, the grief by which we gain God's reward and praise.

Charity uncreated is God. Charity created is our soul in God. Charity given is virtue. This is a gracious gift that works in us so that we love God for himself, and love ourselves in God, and love what God loves for God's sake.

My life was lifted up to heaven and I saw our Lord as a lord in his own house where he had called his much loved friends and servants to a banquet. I saw that the Lord did not sit in one place but ranged throughout the house, filling it with joy and gladness. Completely relaxed and courteous, he was himself the happiness and peace of his dear friends, his beautiful face radiating measureless love like a marvelous symphony.

Though we sin continually he loves us endlessly, and so gently does he show us our sin that we repent of it quietly, turning our mind to the contemplation of his mercy, clinging to his love and goodness, knowing that he is our cure, understanding that we do nothing but sin. If there be anywhere on earth a lover of God who is always kept safe from falling, I know nothing of it—for it was not shown me. But this was shown: that in falling and rising again we are always held close in one love.

I saw with bodily sight into the face of the crucifix before me. There I saw part of Christ's passion: contempt, disgusting spittle, and many drawn out pains, more than I can tell. And in this sight, with all the pains that ever were or ever shall be, I understood the Passion of Christ to be the greatest pain, far surpassing any other. All this was shown to me in an instant of time, and quickly passed over into comfort. For our good Lord did not want the soul to be frightened by this ugly sight.

There were times when I wanted to look away from the cross, but I dared not. For I knew that when I stared at the cross I was safe and sound...Then a friendly suggestion came to my mind, "Look up to heaven toward the Father." But I made an inward answer as firmly as I could and said, "No I cannot. You are my heaven." I said this because I would not look. I would rather endure that suffering until the Day of Judgment than to come to heaven apart from him.

And he said: I may make everything right, I can make all things well, and I shall make all things well; and you shall see for yourself that all manner of things shall be well. When he says, "I may" I understood it to mean the Father; and as he says "I can" I understood the Son; and where he says "I shall" I understood the Holy Spirit; and where he says "You shall see for yourself" I understood the union of all humankind that shall be saved into the Blessed Trinity. In these five words, God wills that we will be enfolded—in rest and peace.

So throughout the vision, I thought I was being obliged to recognize that we are sinners...Yet in spite of all this, I saw that our Lord was never angry; nor would be. For he is God—goodness, life, truth, love, peace. The integrity of his love will not permit him to be angry I saw that it is contrary to his power, his wisdom, and goodness to be angry.

And thus it was that I saw that God rejoices that he is our Father, God rejoices that he is our Mother; and God rejoices that he is our true Spouse, and our soul is his beloved. And Christ rejoices that he is our brother, and Jesus rejoices that he is our Savior. These are the five joys in which he wills that we rejoice: in praising, thanking and enjoying him forever.

How greatly should we rejoice that God indwells our soul! Even more that our soul dwells in God! Our created soul is to be God's dwelling place, and the soul's dwelling place is to be in God, who is uncreated.

Our great Father, God almighty, who is Being, knew and loved us from eternity. Through his knowledge, and in the wonderful depth of his charity, together with the foresight and wisdom of the whole blessed Trinity, he willed that the second Person should be our Mother, Brother, and Savior. Hence it follows that God is as truly our Mother and our Father. Our Father decides, our Mother works, our good Lord, the Holy Spirit, strengthens. So we ought to love our God in whom we have our being.

All things planned before the world began come upon us suddenly, so that in our blindness we say that they are chance. But God knows all. Constantly and lovingly he brings all that happens to its best end. All that is done is well done, for it is done by God.

In times of pain and grief he shows us the joy with which he embraced his own Cross and Passion, at the same time helping us to bear our troubles by his blessed strength. And in times of sin his compassion and pity are there to cheer us, powerfully protecting and defending us against all our enemies. These two are the everyday comforts he shows us in this life. Sometimes a third comfort is mixed with the other two, his blissful joy which is a glimpse of heaven.

Mercy is a work which springs from the goodness of God, and it will continue to work until sin is no longer allowed to molest faithful souls.

The saints in heaven wish to know nothing but what our Lord shows them and furthermore their love and their will is ruled according to our Lord's will. And we therefore ought to exercise our will like them. Then we shall will nothing and desire nothing except the will of our Lord as they do, for we are all one in God's purpose.

And as almighty and as wise as God is to save humanity, so does he will to save them, for Christ himself is the foundation of all the laws by which Christians live and he taught us to do good in return for evil. Here we may see that he is himself this love, and does to us just as he teaches us to do; for he wishes us to be like him in wholeness of endless love to ourselves and to our fellow Christians.

God wishes that we see and enjoy everything in love. But we are most blind about this knowledge, for some of us believe that God is almighty and may do everything, and that he is all wise and is able to do everything, but as for believing that he is all love, there we draw back. And this ignorance is what hinders God's lovers most, as far as I can see.

So our customary practice of prayer was brought to mind: how through our ignorance and inexperience in the ways of love we spend so much time on petition. I saw that it is indeed more worthy of God and more truly pleasing to him that through his goodness we should pray with full confidence, and by his grace cling to him with real understanding and unshakeable love, than that we should go on making as many petitions as our souls are capable of.

And our dying flesh, which the Son of God took upon himself, like Adam's old coat...the Savior transformed into something beautiful, fresh, bright, and splendid, eternally spotless, full and flowing...of a harmony and beauty the like and wonder of which I could never describe.

For the Trinity is God, God is the Trinity; the Trinity is our creator and protector; the Trinity is our everlasting lover, everlasting joy and bliss by our Lord Jesus Christ. And this was shown in the first showing, and in them all; for where Jesus appears the blessed Trinity is understood, as I see it.

It came to my mind that I wanted to have been at that time with Mary Magdalene and with the others who were Christ's lovers and therefore I desired a bodily sight in which I might have more knowledge of the bodily pains of our Savior...the reason I made this petition was so that after the showing I should have a truer awareness of the passion of Christ.

Lord, you know what I want if it be your will that I have it; and if it be not your will, good Lord, be not displeased, for I want nothing which you do not want.

Therefore we may ask from our lover with reverence all that we wish, for our natural will is to have God and the good will of God is to have us. And we may never cease willing or longing until we have him in fullness of joy, and then we will not be able to will anything more, for he wills that we be engaged in knowing and loving until the time when we shall find fulfillment in heaven.

For of all things, gazing at and loving the Creator prompts the soul to appear little in its own sight, and fills it most with reverence, awe and true humility, with much charity towards its fellow Christians.

In my view, this pain exists for a time for it purges and makes us know ourselves and ask for mercy...And for the tender love which our good Lord has for everyone who shall be saved he comforts promptly and sweetly, meaning this: 'It is true that sin is the cause of all this pain, but all shall be well and all manner of thing shall be well.'

May all of us, for charity, pray to God; thanking, trusting, and enjoying in union with the working of God; for our good Lord must be prayed to in this manner according to the understanding that I took in all his own meaning and in the sweet words when he said full merrily, "I am the ground of thy beseeching."

Everything which is done is well done, for our good Lord God does everything; for at this time the working of creatures was not shown to me, but only the operation of God in the creature, for he is the still point at the center and there is no doer but he and I was certain that he does no sin...And in this vision was shown to my understanding, for our Lord wishes that the soul be turned completely to gaze on him and to turn in all particulars from gazing at blind human judgment towards the lovely and sweet judgment of our Lord God.

And at one time my mind was led down to the bottom of the sea, and there I saw green hills and valleys looking as if they were covered with moss...Then I understood this: that if a person were deep under the wide waters, as long as he could still see God—and God is with us always—he should be safe in body and soul and take no harm...for our Lord wills that we believe that we see him all the time continually, even if we feel we can see him very little.

It is God's will that we have three things in our seeking. The first is that we seek willingly and actively, without sloth, as we can through his grace....the second is that we wait on him steadfastly for love, not grumbling, until our life's end—for it lasts so short a time. The third is that we trust him completely with certainty of faith, because this is his will.

And our Lord showed that it is in his Passion that is the fiend's undoing...and as hard as he works, so he continually sees that all the souls of salvation escape him, gloriously, by virtue of Christ's passion. And this is his sorrow, and he is thus put down...For all that God allows him to do turns to joy for us, but it turns to shame and woe to him.

I saw God in a point, that is to say, in my understanding, by which sight I saw that he is everything....Everything which is done is well done, for our Lord God does everything; For at this time the working of creatures was not shown but only the operation of our Lord...for he is the still point at the center...And this vision was shown to my understanding, for our Lord wishes that the soul be turned completely to gaze on him, and to turn in all particulars from gazing at blind human judgment, toward the lovely and sweet judgment of our Lord God.

She [Lady Mary] and Christ were so one in their love that the greatness of her love caused the greatness of her suffering. In this I saw a substance of the kind of love that creatures have toward him, continued by grace. And this human love was most generously and supremely shown in his sweet mother. But just because she loved him more than did anyone else, so much the more did her sufferings transcend theirs.

When a soul holds onto God in trust—whether in seeking him or contemplating him—this is the highest worship it can bring.

Appendix

Aids to Prayer:
Anglican Prayer Beads

Opening prayers for Prayer Beads

First prayer:
Holy Spirit Prayer
Come Holy Spirit, Spirit of love, Spirit of discipline
In the silence:
Come to us and bring us your peace.
Rest in us that we may be tranquil and still,
Speak to us as each needs to hear,
Reveal to us things hidden and things longed for,
Rejoice in us that we may praise and be glad,
Pray in us that we may be at one with you and with each other,
Refresh and renew us from your living springs of water,
Dwell in us now and always. Amen

Or alternately you may use Julian's Prayer:
God of your goodness, give me yourself,
For you are enough to me.
And I can ask for nothing less that is to your glory.
And if I ask for anything less, I shall still be in want, for only in
you have I all.

What are Anglican Prayer Beads?

Anglican Prayer Beads are a relatively new form of prayer, blending the Orthodox Jesus Prayer Rope and the Roman Catholic Rosary. The thirty-three bead design was created by the Rev. Lynn Bauman in the mid-1980s, through the prayerful exploration and discovery of a contemplative prayer group.

The use of the rosary or prayer beads helps to bring us into contemplative of meditative prayer—really thinking about and being mindful of praying, of being in the presence of God—by use of mind, body, and spirit. The touching of the fingers on each successive bead is an aid in keeping our mind from wandering, and the rhythm of the prayers leads us more readily into stillness.

The Prayer Beads comprise four groups of seven beads called Weeks which are divided by four Cruciform beads. The Weeks remind us of the days of Creation, the temporal week, the seasons of the Church year, and the seven Sacraments. The Cruciform beads point to the Cross as the central symbol of our salvation, as well as remind us of the four seasons of the temporal year, and the four points on a compass. A Cross followed by a single Invitatory bead leads one into the circle of prayer of the Beads, similar to the Invitatory (opening psalm) of the Daily Office.

One begins the recitation of the Prayer Beads by holding the Cross and saying the prayer assigned to it, then move to the Invitatory Bead. Then enter the circle of the Beads with the first Cruciform Bead, moving through the Weeks and other Cruciforms, saying the prayers for each bead, and then exiting by way of the Invitatory Bead and Cross. It is suggested that one pray around the circle of beads three times in an unhurried pace, allowing the repetition to become a sort of lullaby of love and praise that enables the mind to rest and the heart to become quiet and still.

When you have completed the round of the prayer beads, you should end with a period of silence. This silence allows you to center your being in an extended period of silence. It also invites reflection and listening after you have invoked the Name and Presence of God.

Where to get prayer beads
Try a google search! You can also make your own:

You need a cross, and either five larger beads and 28 smaller ones. Or the cross with one large bead in one style, four large beads in a second style and 28 smaller beads.

Thread both sides of the strand coming from the cross through the first two large beads. Then on each side, string seven smaller beads, a larger bead and seven smaller beads again. You will have used all but the final larger bead. Put both of the two strands together again, and add the last bead, then tie off with a knot, and cut the string close to the knot.

Symbolism of the Beads

The configuration of the Anglican Prayer Beads relate contemplative prayer using the Rosary to many levels of traditional Christian symbolism. Contemplative prayer is enriched by these symbols whose purpose is always to focus and concentrate attention, allowing the one who prays to move more swiftly into the Presence of God.

The prayer beads are made up of twenty-eight beads divided into four groups of seven called weeks. In the Judeo-Christian tradition the number seven represents spiritual perfection and completion. Between each week is a single bead, called a cruciform bead as the four beads form a cross. The invitatory bead between the cross and the wheel of beads brings the total to thirty-three, the number of years in Jesus' earthly life.

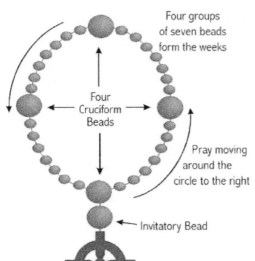

Four groups of seven beads form the weeks

Four Cruciform Beads

Pray moving around the circle to the right

Invitatory Bead

Closing your Prayers
The following ending can be used with any of the prayers in
this booklet. After three circuits around the prayer beads, you
may finish as follows:

Last time through:

Invitatory Bead
The Lord's Prayer

The Cross
I bless the Lord.

Or, in a group setting:
Let us bless the Lord
Thanks be to God.

There are a variety of Prayers that can be used. In the Julian of Norwich Tradition, the following may be said

Julian of Norwich Prayer

The Cross
In the Name of God, Father, Son, and Holy Spirit. Amen.

The Invitatory
O God make speed to save me (us),
O Lord make haste to help me (us),
Glory to the Father, and to the Son, and to the Holy Spirit: As it was in the beginning, is now, and will be forever. Amen.

The Cruciforms
God of your goodness, give me yourself,
For you are enough to me.
And I can ask for nothing less that is to your glory.

And if I ask for anything less, I shall still be in want, for only in you have I all.

The Weeks
All shall be well, and all shall be well,
And all manner of things shall be well.

Or

In His love He has done His works, and in His love He has made all things beneficial to us.

A Form of Prayer based on the Psalter and the Cross

Blessed be the one, holy, and living God.
Glory to God for ever and ever. Amen.

The Invitatory
O God make speed to save me (us),
O Lord make haste to help me (us),
Glory to the Father, and to the Son, and to the Holy Spirit: As
it was in the beginning, is now, and will be forever. Amen.

The Cruciforms
Behold now, bless the Lord, all you servants of the Lord.
You that stand in the house of the Lord, lift up your hands in
the holy place and bless the Lord.

The Weeks
I lift up my eyes to the hills;
From where is my help to come?
My help comes from the Lord,
The maker of heaven and earth.

Using the Orthodox Trisagion and Jesus Prayer

The Cross
In the Name of God, Father, Son, and Holy Spirit. Amen.

The Invitatory
O God make speed to save me (us),
O Lord make haste to help me (us),
Glory to the Father, and to the Son, and to the Holy Spirit: As
it was in the beginning, is now, and will be forever. Amen.

The Cruciforms
Holy God,
Holy and Mighty,
Holy Immortal One,
Have mercy upon me (us).

The Weeks
Lord Jesus Christ, Son of God,
Have mercy on me, a sinner.

Or, in a group setting:
Lord Jesus Christ, Son of God, Have mercy upon us.

Trisagion means "thrice Holy"

Agnus Dei Prayer

The Cross
The Lord's Prayer

The Invitatory
"Let the words of my mouth and the meditation of my heart
be acceptable in your sight, O Lord, my strength and my
redeemer."—Psalm 19:14

The Cruciforms
Oh, Lamb of God that taketh away the sins of the world
have mercy upon us,
Oh, Lamb of God that taketh away the sins of the world
have mercy upon us,

Oh, Lamb of God that taketh away the sins of the world
give us Thy Peace.

The Weeks
Almighty and merciful Lord,
Father, Son, and Holy Spirit,
bless us and keep us.
Amen.

Agnus Dei means "Lamb of God"

A Celtic Form of Prayer

The Cross
In the Name of God, Father, Son, and Holy Spirit. Amen.

The Invitatory
O God make speed to save me (us),
O Lord make haste to help me (us),
Glory to the Father, and to the Son, and to the Holy Spirit: As
it was in the beginning, is now, and will be forever. Amen.

The Cruciforms
Be the eye of God dwelling with me,
The foot of Christ in guidance with me,
The shower of the Spirit pouring on me,
Richly and generously

The Weeks
Pray each phrase on a separate bead.
I bow before the Father who made me,
I bow before the Son who saved me,
I bow before the Spirit who guides me,
In love and adoration.
I praise the Name of the one on high.
I bow before thee Sacred Three,
The ever One, the Trinity.

Come Lord Jesus Prayer

The Cross
"Blessing and glory and wisdom and thanksgiving and honor and power and might be to our God forever and ever! Amen."—Revelation 7:12

The invitatory
"God is our refuge and strength, a very present help in time of trouble."—Psalm 46:1

The Cruciforms
"Bless the Lord, O my soul, and all that is within me, bless God's Holy Name."—Psalm 103:1

The Weeks
"Come Lord Jesus, draw us to yourself."—John 12:32

Saint Patrick's Breastplate

The Cross
I bind unto myself today the strong Name of the Trinity,
by invocation of the same, the Three in One, and One in
Three.
Of whom all nature hath creation, eternal Father, Spirit,
Word:
praise to the Lord of my salvation, salvation is of Christ the
Lord. The Invitatory

Christ be with me, Christ within me, Christ behind me, Christ
before me,
Christ beside me, Christ to win me, Christ to comfort and
restore me.
Christ beneath me, Christ above me, Christ in quiet, Christ in
danger,
Christ in hearts of all that love me, Christ in mouth of friend
and stranger.

The Cruciforms
I bind unto myself today
the strong Name of the Trinity,
by invocation of the same,
the Three in One, and One in Three.

The Weeks
1. I bind this day to me for ever, by power of faith, Christ's
Incarnation;

107

2. his baptism in Jordan river;
3. his death on cross for my salvation;
4. his bursting from the spicèd tomb;
5. his riding up the heavenly way;
6. his coming at the day of doom:
7. I bind unto myself today.

1. I bind unto myself the power of the great love of
cherubim;
2. the sweet "Well done" in judgment hour;
3. the service of the seraphim;
4. confessors' faith, apostles' word,
5. the patriarchs' prayers, the prophets' scrolls;
6. all good deeds done unto the Lord,
7. and purity of virgin souls.

1. I bind unto myself today the virtues of the starlit heaven,
2. the glorious sun's life-giving ray,
3. the whiteness of the moon at even,
4. the flashing of the lightning free,
5. the whirling of the wind's tempestuous shocks,
6. the stable earth, the deep salt sea,
7. around the old eternal rocks.

1. I bind unto myself today the power of God to hold and
lead,
2. his eye to watch, his might to stay,
3. his ear to hearken, to my need;
4. the wisdom of my God to teach,
5. his hand to guide, his shield to ward;
6. the word of God to give me speech,
7. his heavenly host to be my guard.

Form Based on the Anglican Evening Prayer

The Cross
Glory to the Father, and to the Son, and to the Holy Spirit. as
it was in the beginning, is now, and will be for ever. Amen.

The Invitatory
Open my lips, O Lord,
and my mouth shall proclaim
Your praise.

The Cruciforms
Guide us waking, O Lord,
and guard us sleeping;
that awake we may watch
with Christ, and asleep
we may rest in peace.

The Weeks
Jesus, lamb of God, have mercy on us.

"I set my eyes on the same cross in which I had seen comfort before, my tongue to speaking of Christ's Passion and repeating the words of Holy Church, and my heart clinging to God with all my trust and strength" Julian of Norwich, 16th Showing

God of thy goodness give me thyself,
For thou art enough for me. And I can ask for
nothing less that can be, but full honor to thee.
And if I should ever ask anything that is less, ever
shall I be in want.
For only in thee have I all.

Personal Notes

All manner of thing shall be well.

Printed in Great Britain
by Amazon